INTERCESSORY PRAYER ISN'T Pretty!

DR. BARBARA A. PALMER

Kingdom Publishing

INTERCESSORY PRAYER ISN'T PRETTY
The Workbook

Published by:
Kingdom Publishing, LLC
Odenton, MD USA

First printed in the USA

INTERCESSORY PRAYER ISN'T PRETTY!

THE WORKBOOK

A Formation Manual for Trained Intercessors

HOW THIS WORKBOOK IS TO BE USED

This workbook is not a study guide.
It is a training manual.
It is designed to form posture, discipline discernment, and produce obedient intercessors who can function within heaven's situation room with accuracy and endurance.

Intended Use

- Individual formation
- Small-group training cohorts
- Church prayer teams
- Leadership intercession cores

Recommended Pace

- One chapter per week
- Minimum 90–120 minutes of engagement weekly
- Includes prayer practice outside reading time

Formation Outcomes

By the end of this workbook, participants will:

- Discern assignment versus emotional burden
- Shift accurately between worship and intercession
- Recognize spiritual threat levels
- Operate within confidentiality and restraint
- Sustain intercession without burnout
- Respond strategically rather than emotionally

Intercessory Prayer Isn't Pretty
Notes

_____

_____

_____

_____

_____

_____

_____

_____

_____

_____

_____

_____

_____

_____

_____

_____

_____

INTRODUCTION

Intercessory Prayer Is Not Pretty

Formation Theme
Renouncing emotional-driven prayer in favor of disciplined, obedient intercession

Opening Consecration
"Lord, dismantle what I have assumed about intercession. Remove performance, reaction, and emotional dependency. Train me to pray from alignment, not impulse. I surrender my habits so You can form my obedience."

Core Truths (Receive)

- Intercession is responsibility, not expression
- Emotion must respond to revelation, not govern it
- Sound without strategy produces fatigue, not fruit
- Discernment precedes authority

Truth in My Own Words:

_____

_____

_____

Heart Examination (Reflect)

1. Where have I equated intensity with effectiveness?
2. When have I left prayer gatherings emotionally drained but directionless?
3. What part of this introduction unsettled me—and why?

Formation Exercise (Respond)

This Week's Practice

- Before praying, sit in silence for 5 minutes.
- Ask only one question: *"What is the assignment right now?"*
- Pray only what is revealed—no more, no less.

What surfaced:

_____

_____

_____

Group Discussion (If Applicable)

- Why is emotional prayer culture so appealing?
- What risks does it pose to long-term intercessors?

Sealing Prayer

"Lord, retrain me. I choose formation over familiarity. Teach me to carry what You assign—and release what You do not."

CHAPTER 1

Worship Is Not the Target

Formation Theme

Learning to shift from atmosphere into assignment

Core Truths (Receive)

- Worship is the doorway, not the destination
- Lingering without listening prevents authority
- Silence is often the bridge between presence and instruction

Discernment Diagnostic (Reflect)

Rate yourself honestly (1–5):

Statement	1	2	3	4	5
I know when to shift from worship					
I am comfortable with silence					
I wait for instruction before praying					

What do these numbers reveal?

_____

_____

_____

Formation Exercise (Respond)

Practice: The Post-Worship Pause

1. Engage worship intentionally.
2. Stop all sound.
3. Wait until clarity surfaces.
4. Write the assignment.
5. Pray briefly and precisely.

What instruction emerged?

_____

_____

_____

Burden vs Assignment Filter

What I Felt	Was It Assigned?	Scripture Anchor

Accountability (Remain)

- Did I shift when prompted?
- Did silence make me uncomfortable?
- What fruit followed obedience?

Group Discussion

- Why is it difficult to end worship?
- How can leaders help rooms shift without quenching the Spirit?

Sealing Prayer

"Lord, teach me to move when You move. I will not camp in comfort when You are calling for execution."

CHAPTER 2

WHAT ARE YOU AIMING AT?

Formation Theme

Learning to move from vague prayer to targeted intercession

1. OPENING CONSECRATION

"Holy Spirit, deliver me from praying broadly when You are calling for precision. Teach me to pause, discern, and aim. I submit my emotions to Your instruction and my words to Your will."
Sit quietly for 2 minutes.

Ask: "What is the target You want me to see?"

Write what surfaces (if anything):

_____

_____

_____

2. CORE FORMATION TRUTHS (RECEIVE)

- Burden is awareness; assignment is authorization
- Prayer without a target exhausts the intercessor
- Accuracy preserves authority
- Discernment precedes effective warfare
- Scripture sharpens aim

Truth in My Own Words:

_____

_____

3. HEART EXAMINATION (REFLECT)

Answer honestly.

1. Where do I tend to pray emotionally instead of deliberately?
2. What happens in me when I feel burdened but unclear?
3. Have I ever prayed intensely yet felt uncertain afterward about what shifted?

Discernment Inventory

Rate yourself (1 = rarely, 5 = consistently):

Statement	1	2	3	4	5
I pause before praying					
I ask clarifying questions					
I pray Scripture intentionally					
I can articulate what I prayed for					

What patterns do you see?

_____

_____

_____

4. FORMATION EXERCISE (RESPOND)

Practice: Target Identification

Set aside 10 minutes.

1. Sit in silence.
2. Ask: "Holy Spirit, what specifically requires intercession right now?"
3. Wait.
4. Write one clear target only.

Target Identified:

_____

Scripture Alignment:

_____

Prayer (brief, specific):

_____

Burden vs Assignment Table

Burden I Feel	Is This an Assignment?	How Do I Know?

5. OBEDIENCE & ACCOUNTABILITY (REMAIN)

At week's end:

1. Did I pray only what was assigned?
2. Did peace settle after obedience?
3. What changed in my stamina or clarity?

6. GROUP FORMATION (FOR COHORTS)

Discussion Questions

1. Why do we resist specificity in prayer?
2. How does targeting protect intercessors from burnout?
3. What safeguards help groups stay focused?

Group Practice

- Leader identifies one target.
- Group prays one at a time, briefly, in agreement.

7. SEALING PRAYER

"Lord, train my spiritual aim. I will no longer pray randomly. I choose obedience over overflow and accuracy over noise."

Intercessory Prayer Isn't Pretty
Notes

_____

_____

_____

_____

_____

_____

_____

_____

_____

_____

_____

_____

_____

_____

_____

CHAPTER 3

ENTERING THE HOLY OF HOLIES

Formation Theme

Learning to pray from posture, not proximity

1. OPENING CONSECRATION

"Father, take me beyond surface prayer. Teach me reverence, stillness, and submission. I desire instruction more than expression."
Remain silent for 3 minutes.

2. CORE FORMATION TRUTHS (RECEIVE)

- Not all realms of prayer carry the same authority
- Silence is preparation, not inactivity
- Proximity increases responsibility
- Strategy is released in reverence
- Listening precedes speaking

Truth in My Own Words:

_____

_____

_____

3. HEART EXAMINATION (REFLECT)

1. How do I respond to silence in prayer?
2. Do I enter prayer already decided on what I will say?
3. Where might performance be replacing posture?

Realm Awareness Inventory

Statement	Rare	Sometimes	Often	Always
I wait before speaking	☐	☐	☐	☐
I welcome stillness	☐	☐	☐	☐
I receive instruction	☐	☐	☐	☐

What does this reveal about my prayer posture?

_____

_____

4. FORMATION EXERCISE (RESPOND)

Practice: Holy of Holies Discipline

1. Enter prayer with thanksgiving.
2. Stop all speech.
3. Sit quietly until clarity surfaces.
4. Write only what is revealed.
5. Pray it—no additions.

What was revealed:

_____

_____

Revelation Stewardship Check

Insight Received   Was I Tempted to Share?   How Will I Guard It?

_____

5. OBEDIENCE & ACCOUNTABILITY (REMAIN)

End of week reflection:

- Did I rush silence?
- Did I speak more than I listened?
- Did clarity increase when restraint increased?

6. GROUP FORMATION (FOR COHORTS)

Discussion

1. Why is silence uncomfortable in group prayer?
2. How does reverence protect accuracy?

Group Practice
- Five minutes of shared silence before any prayer.
- Leader releases assignment.
- Group prays succinctly.

7. SEALING PRAYER

"Lord, I bow before I speak. I choose reverence over routine. Train me to pray from where You speak."

Intercessory Prayer Isn't Pretty
Notes

_____

_____

_____

_____

_____

_____

_____

_____

_____

_____

_____

_____

_____

_____

_____

_____

_____

CHAPTER 4

HE IS CALLING US HIGHER

Formation Theme

Accepting elevation as responsibility, not status

1. OPENING CONSECRATION

"Lord, lift my perspective above emotion and reaction. I accept the responsibility that comes with elevation."

2. CORE FORMATION TRUTHS (RECEIVE)

- Elevation increases vision, not ego
- Higher realms demand discipline
- Insight often precedes evidence
- Discernment prevents damage
- Authority flows from perspective

Truth in My Own Words:

_____

_____

_____

3. HEART EXAMINATION (REFLECT)

1. Where do I sense God calling me higher?
2. What fears or resistance surface when I consider elevation?
3. Do I associate higher places with isolation or responsibility?

Elevation Readiness Assessment

Indicator	Not Yet	Growing	Consistent
Emotional restraint	☐	☐	☐
Confidentiality	☐	☐	☐
Scriptural grounding	☐	☐	☐
Obedience to promptings	☐	☐	☐

What must mature for elevation to be sustained?

_____

_____

4. FORMATION EXERCISE (RESPOND)

Practice: Elevated Intercession

Ask:

- "What am I being shown before others see it?"
- "What response is required now?"

Insight Received:

_____

Assigned Response:

_____

Emotional Regulation Exercise

When urgency surfaces:

- Pause
- Breathe
- Ask: "Is this alert or anxiety?"

What helped me distinguish the two?

_____

_____

5. OBEDIENCE & ACCOUNTABILITY (REMAIN)

At week's end:

1. Did I react—or intercept?
2. Did I speak prematurely?
3. Did peace accompany obedience?

6. GROUP FORMATION (FOR COHORTS)

Discussion

1. Why does elevation often feel lonely?
2. How does discipline preserve higher perspective?

Group Practice

- Leader shares a hypothetical scenario.
- Group identifies what elevated intercession would look like.

7. SEALING PRAYER

"Father, I accept Your invitation to come higher. Train me to see clearly, speak carefully, and respond faithfully."

Intercessory Prayer Isn't Pretty
Notes

_____

_____

_____

_____

_____

_____

_____

_____

_____

_____

_____

_____

_____

_____

_____

_____

CHAPTER 5

INTIMACY WITH THE HOLY SPIRIT

Formation Theme
Developing responsive intimacy that sustains accurate intercession.

1. OPENING CONSECRATION
"Holy Spirit, I yield my schedule, habits, and preferences to You. Train me to recognize Your voice, respond without delay, and walk in intimacy that produces accuracy."

Sit quietly for 2 minutes.
Do not pray—listen.

2. CORE FORMATION TRUTHS (RECEIVE)

- Intercession cannot exceed intimacy
- Authority is sustained by obedience
- Sensitivity is sharpened through responsiveness
- The Spirit speaks before crisis manifests
- Delay dulls discernment

Truth in My Own Words:

_____

_____

_____

3. HEART EXAMINATION (REFLECT)

Answer prayerfully.

1. How do I normally recognize the Holy Spirit's prompting?
2. What causes me to hesitate or delay obedience?
3. Do I rely more on routine or responsiveness?

Intimacy Inventory
Rate yourself honestly

Statement	Rarely	Sometimes	Often	Always
I respond quickly to promptings	☐	☐	☐	☐
I recognize urgency without panic	☐	☐	☐	☐
I pray beyond scheduled times	☐	☐	☐	☐
I trust the Spirit without explanation	☐	☐	☐	☐

What does this reveal about my intimacy level?

_____

_____

4. FORMATION EXERCISE (RESPOND)

Practice: Prompted Obedience

For the next 7 days:

- Record every prompting you sense.
- Note your response.

Prompting   **Response**   **Outcome**

_____

Reflection:

How did obedience (or delay) affect clarity and peace?

_____

_____

Night Watch Awareness

If awakened unexpectedly:

- Do not dismiss it.
- Pray briefly.
- Ask: "What is required right now?"

What did I learn from this experience?

_____

_____

5. OBEDIENCE & ACCOUNTABILITY (REMAIN)

End of week reflection:

1. Where did intimacy increase?
2. Where did resistance surface?
3. What adjustments must I make to remain sensitive?

6. GROUP FORMATION (FOR COHORTS)

Discussion

1. Why does intimacy disrupt convenience?
2. How does delayed obedience affect group intercession?

Group Practice

- Silent listening (3 minutes)
- Each participant shares only what the Spirit assigned—no commentary.

7. SEALING PRAYER

"Holy Spirit, I choose intimacy over efficiency. Train me to respond quickly, trust deeply, and remain sensitive."

Intercessory Prayer Isn't Pretty
Notes

_____

_____

_____

_____

_____

_____

_____

_____

_____

_____

_____

_____

_____

_____

_____

_____

CHAPTER 6

THE SITUATION ROOM

Formation Theme

Learning discipline, restraint, and confidentiality in strategic intercession

1. OPENING CONSECRATION

"Lord, discipline my tongue, sharpen my discernment, and train me to steward revelation responsibly. I accept the weight of trusted intercession."

2. CORE FORMATION TRUTHS (RECEIVE)

- Intercession is heaven's situation room on earth
- Revelation is for prayer, not exposure
- Confidentiality preserves authority
- Discipline governs effective response
- Silence often protects more than speech

Truth in My Own Words:

_____

_____

3. HEART EXAMINATION (REFLECT)

1. How do I respond when God reveals sensitive information?
2. Do I feel pressure to share insight prematurely?
3. How comfortable am I with restraint?

Confidentiality Readiness Check

Scenario	My Likely Response	Is This Aligned?
God reveals a leader's vulnerability		
I sense danger forming		
I receive insight others don't have		

What must mature in me?

_____

_____

4. FORMATION EXERCISE (RESPOND)

Practice: Situation Room Discipline

Before praying:

1. Identify the threat.
2. Determine the level of urgency.
3. Decide what not to say.
4. Pray precisely.
5. Stop.

Assignment Received:

_____

Prayer Released:

_____

Revelation Stewardship Covenant

Write one sentence committing to guard what God reveals:

_____

_____

_____

5. OBEDIENCE & ACCOUNTABILITY (REMAIN)

End-of-week reflection:

1. Did I guard information well?
2. Did silence increase authority?
3. Did restraint sharpen clarity?

6. GROUP FORMATION (FOR COHORTS)

Discussion

1. Why is confidentiality difficult?
2. How does talking weaken protection?

Group Practice

- Leader presents a scenario.
- Group identifies:
  - What should be prayed
  - What must remain unspoken

7. SEALING PRAYER

"Lord, I will guard what You entrust. I choose discipline over display and obedience over explanation."

Intercessory Prayer Isn't Pretty
Notes

_____

_____

_____

_____

_____

_____

_____

_____

_____

_____

_____

_____

_____

_____

_____

_____

CHAPTER 7

WHY INTERCESSORS NEED ASSIGNMENTS

Formation Theme

Learning to pray within assignment to preserve stamina and authority

1. OPENING CONSECRATION

"Father, deliver me from carrying what You did not assign. Teach me to steward responsibility without overwhelm."

2. CORE FORMATION TRUTHS (RECEIVE)

- Assignment limits scope and increases authority
- Over-carrying leads to burnout
- God never assigns everything to one intercessor
- Clarity preserves endurance
- Obedience sustains longevity

Truth in My Own Words:

_____

_____

_____

3. HEART EXAMINATION (REFLECT)

1. Where have I assumed responsibility God did not give?
2. Do I feel guilty releasing burdens?
3. How do I define faithfulness?

Assignment Clarity Assessment

Area	Assigned	Assumed	Needs Discernment
Family	☐	☐	☐
Church	☐	☐	☐
Leaders	☐	☐	☐
Community	☐	☐	☐

What needs realignment?

_____

_____

_____

4. FORMATION EXERCISE (RESPOND)

Practice: Assignment Confirmation

Ask:

- "What am I authorized to carry?"
- "What must I release?"

Burden Assigned?   **Action**

_____

_____

Release Prayer

Write a prayer releasing unassigned burdens:

_____

_____

5. OBEDIENCE & ACCOUNTABILITY (REMAIN)

End-of-week reflection:

1. Did clarity increase peace?
2. Did releasing burdens increase stamina?
3. How did obedience affect endurance?

6. GROUP FORMATION (FOR COHORTS)

Discussion

1. Why do intercessors over-carry?
2. How does assignment protect longevity?

Group Practice

- Each participant shares one assignment they are stewarding.
- Group affirms—not adds to—the assignment.

7. SEALING PRAYER

"Lord, I accept what You assign and release what You do not. Teach me to pray faithfully, not excessively."

Intercessory Prayer Isn't Pretty
Notes

_____

_____

_____

_____

_____

_____

_____

_____

_____

_____

_____

_____

_____

_____

_____

CHAPTER 8

DEFCON INTERCESSION LEVELS

Formation Theme

Learning to discern levels of threat and respond without panic

1. OPENING CONSECRATION

"Father, deliver me from reactionary prayer. Train me to discern levels, timing, and response. I choose discernment over drama and obedience over urgency."

Sit quietly for 2 minutes.

Ask: "What level of response is required right now?"

2. CORE FORMATION TRUTHS (RECEIVE)

- Not every burden is an emergency
- Heaven does not respond to every threat the same way
- Discernment prevents overreaction and under-response
- Wrong posture weakens authority
- Accurate response preserves endurance

Truth in My Own Words:

_____

_____

_____

3. HEART EXAMINATION (REFLECT)

1. Do I tend to treat every burden as urgent?
2. How do I respond when pressure increases?
3. Have I confused intensity with importance?

Response Pattern Inventory

Situation	My Usual Response	Was It Proportionate
Sudden urgency		
Ongoing pressure		
Emotional heaviness		

What patterns emerge?

_____

_____

4. FORMATION EXERCISE (RESPOND)

DEFCON Discernment Practice

Identify the level:

- DEFCON 5: Watchful awareness
- DEFCON 4: Heightened alert
- DEFCON 3: Focused intercession
- DEFCON 2: Intensified response
- DEFCON 1: Immediate, sustained intercession

Situation Discerned:

_____

Level Identified:

_____

Response Required:

_____

_____

Posture Alignment Check

Level	My Posture	Adjustment Needed

5. OBEDIENCE & ACCOUNTABILITY (REMAIN)

End-of-week reflection:

1. Did discernment reduce anxiety?
2. Did correct posture preserve strength?
3. Did peace follow obedience?

6. GROUP FORMATION (FOR COHORTS)

Discussion

1. Why do intercessors overreact?
2. How does misreading threat levels cause burnout?

Group Practice

- Leader presents a scenario.
- Group discerns level before praying.

7. SEALING PRAYER

"Lord, I will respond—not react. I accept Your discipline and trust Your timing."

Intercessory Prayer Isn't Pretty
Notes

_____

_____

_____

_____

_____

_____

_____

_____

_____

_____

_____

_____

_____

_____

_____

_____

CHAPTER 9

ROLES WITHIN THE INTERCESSOR SITUATION ROOM

Formation Theme

Understanding function, restraint, and cooperation in corporate intercession

1. OPENING CONSECRATION

"Lord, position me according to function, not preference. Teach me to serve faithfully within the role You assign."

2. CORE FORMATION TRUTHS (RECEIVE)

- Not all intercessors function the same
- Role clarity strengthens unity
- Overstepping weakens authority
- Cooperation multiplies effectiveness
- Humility sustains trust

Truth in My Own Words:

_____

_____

_____

3. HEART EXAMINATION (REFLECT)

1. Do I struggle when I am not leading?
2. How do I respond to authority in prayer settings?
3. Have I ever overstepped my role?

Role Discernment Inventory

Role	Resonates	Requires Growth
Watchman	☐	☐
Strategist	☐	☐
Sustainer	☐	☐
Guardian	☐	☐

What does this reveal about my function?

_____

_____

4. FORMATION EXERCISE (RESPOND)

Practice: Functional Submission

Ask:

- "What is my role in this assignment?"
- "Who am I supporting?"

Role Identified:

_____

Action Required:

_____

Cooperation Reflection

Situation	Did I Stay in Role?	Outcome

5. OBEDIENCE & ACCOUNTABILITY (REMAIN)

End-of-week reflection:

1. Did role clarity reduce confusion?
2. Did humility increase effectiveness?
3. Did unity strengthen authority?

6. GROUP FORMATION (FOR COHORTS)

Discussion

1. Why is role clarity essential in intercession?
2. How does competition weaken prayer teams?

Group Practice

- Assign roles for a mock scenario.
- Each intercessor functions only within their role.

7. SEALING PRAYER

"Father, I choose function over visibility. Position me where I serve best."

Intercessory Prayer Isn't Pretty
Notes

_____

_____

_____

_____

_____

_____

_____

_____

_____

_____

_____

_____

_____

_____

_____

INTERCESSORY PRAYER ISN'T PRETTY

CHAPTER 10

QUESTIONS EVERY INTERCESSOR MUST ANSWER

Formation Theme

Embracing accountability, maturity, and self-governance in intercession

1. OPENING CONSECRATION

"Lord, search me. Remove immaturity, presumption, and self-deception. I invite Your correction so I may be trusted."

2. CORE FORMATION TRUTHS (RECEIVE)

- Intercession requires self-examination
- Authority flows from alignment
- God trusts accountable intercessors
- Maturity requires honest assessment
- Responsibility precedes expansion

Truth in My Own Words:

_____

_____

_____

3. HEART EXAMINATION (REFLECT)

Answer slowly and honestly.

1. Why has God trusted me with intercession?
2. What patterns threaten my effectiveness?
3. Where do I resist correction?

Core Intercessor Questions

Question	My Honest Answer
Can I be trusted with silence?	
Do I respond or react?	
Do I pray to be heard or to enforce?	
Am I submitted to authority?	

4. FORMATION EXERCISE (RESPOND)

Practice: Alignment Audit

Ask the Holy Spirit:

"What must change for me to be trusted with more?"

Correction Identified:

_____

Adjustment Required:

_____

Growth Commitment

Write one specific commitment for maturation:

_____

_____

5. OBEDIENCE & ACCOUNTABILITY (REMAIN)

End-of-week reflection:

1. Did honesty produce freedom?
2. Did correction sharpen clarity?
3. Did humility increase trust?

6. GROUP FORMATION (FOR COHORTS)

Discussion

1. Why do intercessors avoid self-examination?
2. How does accountability protect calling?

Group Practice

- Silent reflection.
- Each participant writes (does not share) one correction God revealed.

7. SEALING PRAYER

"Lord, I choose maturity. I accept correction so I can be trusted."

Intercessory Prayer Isn't Pretty
Notes

_____

_____

_____

_____

_____

_____

_____

_____

_____

_____

_____

_____

_____

_____

_____

_____

CHAPTER 11
A PRAYER FOR THE INTERCESSOR

Formation Theme

Receiving strengthening, covering, and renewal for sustained intercession

1. OPENING CONSECRATION

"Father, I come to You not to give, but to receive. Strengthen what You have formed. Heal what has been strained. Cover what You have entrusted to me."

Remain still for 2 minutes.

Breathe slowly. Allow your body to settle.

2. CORE FORMATION TRUTHS (RECEIVE)

- Intercessors require intentional strengthening
- Prayer is not only something we do—it is something we receive
- God covers those He assigns
- Renewal preserves longevity
- Grace sustains obedience over time

Truth in My Own Words:

_____

_____

_____

3. HEART EXAMINATION (REFLECT)

1. Where have I been weary in intercession?
2. What parts of my prayer life feel strained or neglected?
3. Do I allow God to minister to me—or only through me?

Weariness Awareness Inventory

Area	Strong	Fatigued	Needs Renewal
Spiritual	☐	☐	☐
Emotional	☐	☐	☐
Mental	☐	☐	☐
Physical	☐	☐	☐

What needs intentional care?

_____

_____

4. FORMATION EXERCISE (RESPOND)

Practice: Receiving Prayer

Read the prayer from Chapter 11 of the book slowly, aloud.

After reading:

- Sit quietly.
- Do not analyze.
- Allow God to minister.

What did I sense God restoring or reaffirming?

_____

Strengthening Declaration (Write Your Own)

_____

5. OBEDIENCE & ACCOUNTABILITY (REMAIN)

End-of-week reflection:

1. Did I allow myself to rest without guilt?
2. Did renewal increase clarity?
3. What practices helped restore strength?

6. GROUP FORMATION (FOR COHORTS)

Group Practice

- Read the prayer aloud together.
- Sit in silence for 3 minutes.
- No discussion—only reception.

Discussion (Afterward)

1. Why is it difficult for intercessors to receive?
2. How does strengthening protect longevity?

7. SEALING PRAYER

"Lord, thank You for covering me. I receive Your strengthening and commit to stewarding my calling with wisdom and rest."

Intercessory Prayer Isn't Pretty
Notes

_____

_____

_____

_____

_____

_____

_____

_____

_____

_____

_____

_____

_____

_____

CHAPTER 12

FINAL CHARGE – WE WILL ALWAYS BE IN THE SITUATION ROOM

Formation Theme

Accepting lifelong responsibility as a trained and trusted intercessor

1. OPENING CONSECRATION

"Lord, I accept the responsibility of what You have shown me. I choose faithfulness over novelty and obedience over emotion."

2. CORE FORMATION TRUTHS (RECEIVE)

- Intercession is not seasonal—it is ongoing stewardship
- Trained intercessors remain watchful
- Responsibility does not expire with comfort
- Faithfulness is often unseen
- God trusts those who endure

Truth in My Own Words:

_____

_____

_____

3. HEART EXAMINATION (REFLECT)

1. How has my understanding of intercession changed?
2. What responsibilities am I now more aware of?
3. Am I willing to remain faithful without recognition?

Readiness Assessment

Statement	Not Yet	Growing	Established
I understand my assignment	☐	☐	☐
I can discern posture shifts	☐	☐	☐
I guard revelation	☐	☐	☐
I sustain discipline	☐	☐	☐

What must continue developing?

_____

_____

_____

4. FORMATION EXERCISE (RESPOND)

Practice: Situation Room Commitment

Write a brief commitment statement describing how you will remain vigilant, disciplined, and obedient.

_____

_____

_____

Responsibility Mapping

Area of Responsibility	How I Will Remain Faithful
Assignment	
Discernment	
Confidentiality	
Endurance	

5. OBEDIENCE & ACCOUNTABILITY (REMAIN)

End-of-week reflection:

1. Do I see intercession as a calling, not a moment?
2. What safeguards will I maintain?
3. Who helps hold me accountable?

6. GROUP FORMATION (FOR COHORTS)

Discussion

1. Why does endurance matter more than intensity?
2. How does unseen faithfulness protect communities?

Group Practice

- Each participant writes a private commitment.
- Leader prays a commissioning prayer.

7. SEALING PRAYER

"Lord, I accept my place in Your situation room. Train me to remain watchful, obedient, and faithful for as long as You entrust me."

Intercessory Prayer Isn't Pretty
Notes

_____

_____

_____

_____

_____

_____

_____

_____

_____

_____

_____

_____

_____

_____

_____

_____

CONCLUSION

TRAINED, TRUSTED, AND POSITIONED

Formation Theme

Integrating formation into lifelong practice

1. FINAL REFLECTION

Take time to reflect across the entire journey.
1.   What has shifted most in my understanding of intercession?
2.   What disciplines must I protect?
3.   What warning signs will I watch for?

2. FORMATION SUMMARY

Complete the following statements:

- Intercession is no longer…
- Intercession now requires…
- God has trained me to…

3. COVENANT OF STEWARDSHIP

Write and sign a personal covenant committing to disciplined intercession.

Signature: _____

Date: _____

4. COMMISSIONING PRAYER

"Father, thank You for training these intercessors. Guard what You have formed. Preserve their endurance. Trust them with what others cannot see. May they stand faithfully between heaven and earth, praying accurately, responding obediently, and remaining steadfast until Your will is fulfilled."